Poems of Nature and Despair

poems by

Marc Petrie

Finishing Line Press
Georgetown, Kentucky

Poems of Nature and Despair

To Amy Greyson, Sammy Petrie

Copyright © 2021 by Marc Petrie
ISBN 978-1-64662-509-3 First Edition
All rights reserved under International and Pan-American Copyright Conventions. No part of this book may be reproduced in any manner whatsoever without written permission from the publisher, except in the case of brief quotations embodied in critical articles and reviews.

ACKNOWLEDGMENTS

Grateful acknowledgments to the following literary journals where some of the poems in this book have been published:

"Red Granite" appeared in *OnTheBus*, 1995.
"Forgiven" appeared in *Spillway*, 1997.
"View from Rock Cabin" appeared in *Then All Goes Blue*, Pacific Writers' Press, 1997.
Mourning on a Deserted Beach" appears in the upcoming issue of *Book of Matches*, 2021.

I would like to thank my wife and son, the other poets I have worked with over the years many of whom are no longer with us; Jerry Palley, Terri Brindt Joseph, Steve Kowit, Jose Antonio Burciaga, and Sam Hammill. I would also like to thank Alejandro Morales, Ute Marguerie Seine, Donna Hilbert, Thelma Reyna, Jack Grapes, and the larger community of poets who have helped me over the years.

Special Acknowledgement to Thelma Reyna and Alejandro Morales for their support through this project.

Publisher: Leah Huete de Maines
Editor: Christen Kincaid
Cover Art: Marc Petrie
Author Photo: Marc Petrie
Cover Design: Elizabeth Maines McCleavy

Printed in the USA on acid-free paper.
Order online: www.finishinglinepress.com
         also available on amazon.com

Author inquiries and mail orders:
Finishing Line Press
P. O. Box 1626
Georgetown, Kentucky 40324
U. S. A.

Table of Contents

A confession 1

The dawning of Aquarius 2

Patience 3

Mallarmé meets Virgil 4

Roaming the rooftops 5

A New Birth 6

Becoming truly literate 7

Why I love this land, in muted silence 8

South of the Sur 9

On Santa Cruz Island, 2018 10

Red Granite 11

Intimate Landscape 12

Three days from nowhere 13

Incident at Forest Falls 14

On a photo shot in a high school journalism class, 1971 15

Vous avez le droit de faire ça vous savez 16

CNN—April 16, 2003 17

The biggest heartache is loneliness 18

Notes on therapy 19

Atlantic Dawn 20

On the beach 22

Days of Awe 23

View from Rock Cabin 24

Mourning on a deserted beach 25

November 25, 1996 26

Forgiven 27

and that around this lament-world, even as
around the other earth, a sun revolved
and a silent star-filled heaven, a lament-
heaven, with its own, disfigured stars.

> *Orpheus. Eurydice. Hermes*
> Rainer Maria Rilke
> Translated by Stephen Mitchell

Introduction

I spent time tracing the limits of symmetry recently. I stood atop a 700-foot cliff at the edge of the ocean where I watched the scalloped waves push ashore, listened to the ocean roar with its fading doppler effect, looked at rounded cliffs covered with immense forests fade into the sea at the southern limit of the horizon, and watched a basaltic tongue create a trough that captured and contained the repetitive power of ocean waves.

I defy those who separate math and science from literature and art. I never dreamed myself a math teacher forty years ago. And here I stand today. I dreamt myself a writer, a novelist. Forty years later I am going through a formal edit.

People say we diminish with age. That's not how I see it. I no longer rely on my physical self or quickness as much. I have moved into more cerebral realms that require slow deep thinking: teaching, fatherhood, poetry, novels.

I won't say I enjoy aging. I hope to be a child, even a motherless child, all of my days. I can find joy in the process of aging, and channel that joy to success, as much as I give it half a chance, as distant as I dare to leap.

The poems in this chapbook channel nature through despair into joy. We all have to weave a path through that tunnel to make it to the light.

I hope you enjoy my work as much as I enjoy sharing it with you.

A confession

I admit I excel
at beating myself up.

I've had lots of practice:
Confusion—to—Dread Fear,

a sense of listing,
unable to right my own hull.

I call this sensation
drowning in air.

The dawning of Aquarius

In 1969,
the balance
between earth and fire
slipped away.

Pure water
drained
from
the Globe.

Sea birds
smothered
in spilled tar.

Children
fled Napalm
naked in fear.

Astronauts
kicked up
moon dust

We saw
the earth
in space:

a blue pill
swallowed
by darkness.

Patience

Patience, like
the roots of a tree,
forsakes the stones
turned over
by the 20th century
as it sinks
roots deeper
in the earth.

Mallarmé meets Virgil

Deep underground,
fire settles

on the surface
of black water.
In the sky

the conjunction

of crescent moon,
Venus,
Jupiter

hover:

above the sea
one step
from disaster.

Mallarmé

Is a butcher.
I find myself
in need of meat.

DID YOU NOT LISTEN

I said before.
The darkness
suits me.

Roaming the rooftops

Perhaps, just maybe
there is a place in this world
where I can let go of this turmoil.

No lightning rods
gather these feelings.
I've walked alone
on too many rooftops.

Listen:

The intense tapping of rain
against the red tiles.
Rest safe inside.
Let the storm run its course.

A New Birth
December 29, 1997

The back of my eyes
fill
with all of life's
glory.

Out of the whale's
mouth
came Jonah.
Rejoice.

How will you
greet this day?

When the sun
has run
its course
through all
the signs of heaven

Will you
sleep
with despair or delight?

When blankets
cover you
will you sleep
the long night through,

focused on the stars,
the nebulae,
the dry flat world
which stretches out before you?

Blue lakes
bordered by pines
shimmer.

Oceans
stretch beyond
the sunlight in your eyes.

Becoming truly literate

My son curled on the couch,
The house agreeably quiet,
In my silent self
I watch my six-year-old sleep.
I would like to learn
How not to read.

Why I love this land, in muted silence

Thunderheads
clear
around
the peak.

Soft, white
clouds
halo
the saddle.

Glaciers
flow
severe white
to the southwest.

Darker clouds
pick up
the trail
of the sun

west of the ridge line
where skies
fade
to light blue.

Celestial mastheads
diminish the continent
as daylight at long last
dies.

South of the Sur

I borrowed
a horn
from the fabulous
siren.

We shared a ride.
It sat in the
passenger seat.

Beyond
Piedras Blancas,
the white rocks
south of the Sur,

it answered
the turbulent
call of the sea.

On Santa Cruz Island, 2018

A clarity exists
in nature
lost
In civilization.

I can't see
eye-to-eye
with the raven.

The bald eagle
nests
along the edge
of a cliff—a

precipitous
drop
to
the sea.

The eagle
dives the length,
plunges talons into fish
to feed its young.

The raven
focuses on
eagle's nest
empty—

Except for
hatchlings
left unguarded.

Red Granite

Beyond the wars
Beyond the rising smog
Far from the lingering hate
Past the urban blight
Red light
Shines
On a sheer granite face
Somewhere
In the Sierra.

Intimate Landscape

Monsoon stopped.
A patch of mesa
shines ochre.

Brilliant light
just under the cloud
splits into
small spectral colors

growing
brighter in hue,
sharper in intensity

until
that small segment
becomes

the purest rainbow
cast against
the deep red mesa.

On car radio
Deep Purple
sings 'Hush.'

Three days from nowhere

Air breaks in blue waves:
deepest, driest azure
Sonoran Desert turquoise;

a shade that speaks
of unbreakable drought,
a dry that vanquishes thirst.

To the east, afternoon heat
boils huge cumulous—
white scoops of sundae clouds

rich with moisture.
Ready to drip vanilla rain
on the parched earth.

That ultimate formation drifts off
never to unload its flood gates here.
Its underside filled with

dust, thunder, and lightening
a terrifying darkness.
I don't want to cover me.

This harsh blue atmosphere
crackles with dryness
over unmarked territory.

Pure white rises
skyward out of the reach
of my outstretched arm.

Coastal winds
carry them westward,
the other side of the ridge.

Relief will come this way
as long as my tongue
will not evaporate,
My eyes will not dry.

Incident at Forest Falls

When I skipped across
Mills Creek Sunday afternoon,
the lustrous sand
in the murky water
clung to my shoes
like a serpent's tongue.

The skies opened:
in green grasses, covered
by my poncho
I counted quartzites in river rock
that covered cracks where snakes hid
until the cloudburst passed.

That day a man drowned
in the channel at Forest Falls
caught in a flash flood.
The firemen pulled out his body
several miles downstream.

On a photo shot in a high school journalism class, 1971

Before I knew things weren't right:
before the years of abuse
by myself and others
took their toll,

before this face looked back
with eyes half-shut by fatigue
lined by crowfeet drawn in pain,

I was Marc Petrie—
the quiet anger looking up
at the black-and-white world:
blind to the colors that surrounded me.

Those eyes once filled with fire
a rebel who wanted nothing
and wanted it all.

Never becoming who I thought I'd be,
I am left with who I became—
a father, a husband,
a man who learned to love.

Vous avez le droit de faire ça vous savez

It was night all morning long.
The sun was shining
And it was going to shine.
A microwave tower sat
Atop the green hillside.

A giant octopus washed up
Along the seashore.
Each dead arm held
Its own fountain pen.

No one is writing.
Everyone carries a torch.
The octopus gets lost in darkness,
Which has no place in the light.

CNN—April 16, 2003

The war is subsiding
Into a pleasant coma
Of lootings,
religious assassinations,
And other assorted acts
Of uncivil disobedience
While the uniformed liberators
Are content to stand
Around the perimeter
of the square
And contain the carnage.

The biggest heartache is loneliness

The bare branches
of a pruned tree
reach for the sky.
Even dormant,
new buds are forming.
A single crow roosts.

Notes on therapy

Hot on the cusp
Of deepened emotions
Anger and cruelty
A breakthrough
In intimacy
The close fit of stones
In a Mayan arch
Held together
By gravity.

Translate the clouds
Into Billowing galleys
Manned by Virgil and Dante
We float downstream
Into the underworld
Where deep blue hell beckons
Before I return
From my indigo swim
Into the twilight.

The ground beneath
My bed settles to a state
Of repose. I return to
The body I left,
Hear my love's breath
Upon the pillow,
Open my eyes in terror, and
Pull the covers tight
Around my heart.

Atlantic Dawn

The ocean reflects
the sky like a bowl
of floating camellias.
Small perfect waves flower
Barely break the placidity
Of the surface

In blue, rose, orange,
and the steel-gray
That comes of nothing.
Tails of range fire
Trail off where water meets sand:
The hues quiver, mix in an image

Distributed by small perfect waves
That distend the globe,
Then remake it again.
The marigold sun appears
above a bank of soft clouds.
Tendrils of light burst

to paint the day.
Pink light thrown out
like petals
showers the sky
with a path for the living.
Colors melt together

In the soft sand
As clouds become
The same shade as the void,
Almost frozen in time
They merge into nothing:
Illuminating all the world

Until the pen in my hand
Becomes nothing,
the sand on which I sit
becomes nothing,
Waves break onshore
With confident self-assurance

To whisper 'you are no more.'

On the beach

We walk on a perfect beach.
I just emerged from
the curl of an 8-foot wave
which I rode forever.

My wife is smiling.
She has never had and
will never have cancer.

Our son dribbles
a soccer ball
with sound knees

A pod of dolphins breaks the waves.

Days of Awe

A fissure forms
In the firmament tonight.
Leafless trees grow luminous
Between the rising hoarfrost
And the clear, dark sky.
I shiver as the cold mist rises.
The yellowed meadow grass
Soaks the toes of my boots
It is almost too cold to bear.
Yet stars sparkle overhead
And the frost casts
Its ghostly presence
Across the autumn meadow.
I lean against the wooden fence
Silent as a cliff.

View from Rock Cabin

I see where
Purple lupine
climb slopes
toward the stars

where water flows
downhill
through flowers.

A blue jay
Squawks its way
Up a pine.

Beyond the lupines
Blue fissures crack clouds
where Redwood trees
rise above

Atwater creek.
Daisies sway
In clefts on cliffs.

The lupine
light a path
To heaven.

If I were climb them
To the stars
I would know
The face of God.

That would break
My covenant
With the lupines'
Bleeding purple hearts

Where a river sprays off
rock near the headwater.
A million trees
lay before me.

Mourning on a deserted beach
December 25, 2015; Two weeks after my mother's death

A steady breeze—
Bright sun—
I close my eyes
to any new light.

The glare
does not hide
dark, cupped
Shadows.

White gulls
above palisades
distract me.

A wind rises
above the surf:

All this world's
remnants
remind me
I am still alive.

November 25, 1996
Yosemite Lodge, California

I experience a tactile
Sense of dread
In the mountains
Each nightfall.

It is past sunset:
Sunset at four-thirty-five
Quick mountain darkness,
Dark by five.

I hiked to Vernal Falls
From Sentinel Bridge
Late this afternoon.

Most of the late afternoon
Alpen glow already faded
By the time I returned
To the Happy Isles.

I was too tired to enjoy it,
Though I got two
Walk-stopping views
On the way to Yosemite Falls.

I was tired when
I boarded the shuttle.
It was dark when the bus
Reached Yosemite Village

And I was filled with
The gloom of nightfall.

Forgiven

Michigan, an emerald icicle
Its aching lawn rolling
Into eternity,

an ancient
gravel pit
filled with water.

Dive in
Avoid
the spiked bottom.

Broken dreams
Never remain.
An Unhinged
Iron work door squeaks.

Grand clouds float in the sky.
I long to float
But instead take the dive.

The quarry floor is lined
With impaled butterflies
Crippled forget-me-nots.
'
They lead into the dark basement
Hear the pinched body of baby crying
A living black-and-blue baby:
My sister.

Those day are gone.
Perpetrators wear heavenly smiles.
Life floats in clouds

Ice cream reflections
 Dark streaks—Chocolate marbling
The quivering surface
Of the gravel pit.

A sign is planted
in the great green lawn
'Come home' the sign reads
'All is forgiven.'

Marc Petrie has been a quiet voice in poetry for the past 25 years. His writing credit for a 1996 publication in City Lights Review typifies his anonymity: "Marc Petrie appeared on the transom with no clue to his whereabouts." His poems have been featured on APM's Writer's Almanac. His poems have appeared in a number of journals over the years including *City Lights Review, Pearl, California State Poetry Review, ONTHEBUS*, and *The Wire*. He has published a chapbook, *The Orange Love Spoon*, Laguna Poets Press, 1998, and *Then All Goes Blue*, 1996. He recently published his first novel, *A Dream Once Dreamed*. He was a board member of Orange County PEN and a member of the Los Angeles Poetry Collective and the Laguna Poets. He organized readings for Orange County PEN and other Orange County poetry groups. His book *Then All Goes Blue* is in both the Yosemite National Park Library and the Mineral King Ranger Station at Mineral King in Sequoia National Park.

Following the birth of his son in 1997, Petrie took a step back from active publication to help raise his son and coach soccer. He focused on raising his son. In 2003, at age 50, Petrie switched his career from engineering to education. He received teaching credentials in elementary education, math, and French, and has been teaching middle school in Santa Ana California since 2008, where he was teacher of the year in 2018. Although he did not actively try to publish he continued his writing. He has written every day since July 1, 1990. He holds a Master of Systems Management from the Viterbi School of Engineering at the University of Southern California and a Bachelor of Arts Degree from the University of California San Diego. He wrote for three college newspapers, the U.S.C. *Daily Trojan*, the U.C.L.A. *Daily Bruin*, and the U.C.S.D. *Daily Triton*. Petrie has lived in Tustin for 30 years with his wife Amy. His son is a student at California State University, Channel Islands.

www.ingramcontent.com/pod-product-compliance
Lightning Source LLC
LaVergne TN
LVHW041507070426
835507LV00012B/1400